The Battle of
Bannockburn
1314

Oliver Hayes

Acknowledgements

Photos, illustrations and maps are by the publisher except:
Statue of king Robert the Bruce in front of Marischal College, L E X commons;
Statue of Robert the Bruce at Stirling Castle, Christian Bickel;
Tomb of Sir James Douglas, GFDL

Website - www.BretwaldaBooks.com
Twitter - @Bretwaldabooks
Facebook - Bretwalda Books
Blog - bretwaldabooks.blogspot.co.uk/

Bretwalda Books
Unit 8, Fir Tree Close, Epsom,
Surrey KT17 3LD
info@BretwaldaBooks.com
www.BretwaldaBooks.com
ISBN 978-1-909698-89-5

CONTENTS

Chapter 1
The Scottish Wars of Independence

T he war that climaxed with the stunning Scottish victory at Bannockburn in 1314 had it origins in 1290 when Queen Margaret of Scotland died leaving no close relatives to inherit the crown. No fewer than 13 Scottish nobles announced that they were the rightful King of Scotland and for a while it looked as if civil war might break out. To avoid this catastrophe the Scottish nobles made a decision that would plunge Scotland into an even worse series of wars: they asked King Edward I of England to study the competing claims and decide who should be the next King of Scotland.

Edward I was not the sort of man to allow an opportunity to pass him by. He chose John Balliol to be king, but only after extracting from Balliol a promise that he would recognise Edward as his overlord. Balliol agreed readily enough, such agreements being not uncommon in medieval Europe. He expected his duties to England to be relatively light, but Edward chose to treat King John of Scotland as if he were a subject who had no more power or rights than an English farmer. Edward issued orders, sent instructions and appointed officials, ignoring King John's views or wishes.

In July 1295 the Scots agreed a treaty with France without consulting Edward, who promptly invaded. John Balliol was captured and imprisoned in the Tower of London. Edward declared that he was now ruling Scotland himself and set about installing his own men in positions of power. The Englishmen did not behave well and several atrocities were committed.

Unsurprisingly an uprising against English rule quickly broke out. Led by a relatively obscure knight named William Wallace the rising achieved success at the Battle of Stirling Bridge in 1297, but Edward struck back at the Battle of Falkirk the following year. Thereafter the fighting raged back and forth with neither side managing to secure a final victory. Wallace was captured in 1305 and Edward had him charged with treason. "I could not be a traitor to Edward, for I was never his subject," responded Wallace, but Edward had him executed in the

4

most painful and barbarous manner anyway. If Edward hoped Wallace's death would end the Scottish uprising he was wrong. Scottish leadership merely passed into other hands.

A turning point came in 1306 when two of the leading claimants to the Scottish throne met at Dumfries. In circumstances that remain unclear Robert Bruce stabbed John Comyn to death. Bruce then openly declared that he was King of Scotland and summoned all true Scots to join him in a war of liberation against the English. The Comyns and their allies denounced Bruce as a murderer and joined the English cause. Other Scottish families were at first equally ambivalent, but over time most came to support Robert Bruce. The death of Edward I of England was a boost to Bruce. Many Scottish knights and nobles who had sworn oaths to Edward now felt that they were free to act as they wished. Moreover, Edward's successor as King of England, his son Edward II, turned out to be interested in neither Scotland nor in warfare.

The statue of William wallace at Aberdeen. The statue was erected in 1888 and bears this inscription: I tell you a truth, liberty is the best of all things, my son, never live under any slavish bond.

By the spring of 1314 Bruce had managed to defeat the English in Scotland. Through a carefully planned and brilliantly executed guerrilla campaign he had worn down the English strength to almost nothing. Key fortresses were captured one by one, patrols were ambushed, supplies destroyed until finally only the impregnable fortress of Stirling Castle remained in English hands. The castle was besieged by Edward Bruce, younger brother of Robert. He agreed with the castle's commander, Sir Thomas Mowbray, that the castle would surrender on 25 June, unless it had been relieved. Such agreements were common in medieval warfare. They reduced casualties on both sides and satisfied chivalric honour.

Robert Bruce was furious when he heard of the agreement. He had been hoping to starve Stirling into surrender and so secure all of Scotland under his rule. Now that such an obvious challenge had been thrown down he knew that King Edward II of England was bound to march into Scotland with a large army. Edward II reacted exactly as Robert Bruce had feared, announcing that he was marching to relieve Stirling with a mighty army.

For Edward II, the invasion of Scotland went wrong right from the start. He ordered that his feudal host was to muster at Berwick upon Tweed by 11 June at the very latest. In his haste, however, he had not summoned Parliament to vote

Stirling Castle from the south. The Battle of Bannockburn was fought as the English sought to relieve their garrison trapped in Stirling Castle by Edward Bruce, younger brother of King Robert Bruce.

the money to pay for the expedition. This not only left him short of cash to pay for supplies and wages, but it also gave those who opposed Edward the excuse they needed not to attend. Several leading noblemen, including four earls, and many others did not turn up, thus depriving Edward of some much-needed military experience.

Nevertheless, it was a large army that Edward gathered together. We do not know exactly how many men Edward had, but he seems to have had about 1,000 heavily armoured cavalry - knights, esquires and mounted men-at-arms. One commission of array, that sent to York, has survived. In it the Mayor of York is instructed to send infantry only as cavalry would be of little use in the forests and marshes near to Stirling where it was expected any battle would be fought. It therefore seems likely that the English army had a disproportionately large number of infantry. Assuming Edward summoned the arrays of the northern shires in the same proportion as York, plus the feudal levies of that area, he may have summoned some 21,000 men.

However, the commissions were not sent out until 27 May, allowing only two weeks for the men to gather and march to Berwick. It is unlikely that they all got there on time. We have no surviving records of the numbers of men who actually joined the army. In addition to the 1,000 or so cavalry, there may have been as many as 17,000 infantry, but there may equally as well have been only around 9,000. That Edward did not have as many men as he expected can be deduced by the fact that he waited until 17 June before setting off, leaving himself barely enough time to march the 98 miles to Stirling, never mind fight a campaign on the way.

The English army crossed the Tweed at Wark, struck northwest to Lauder and then crossed the Lammermuir Hills to reach Edinburgh. Both city and castle were in Scottish hands, so Edward skirted both and headed up the valley of the Forth by way of Linlithgow and Falkirk to approach Stirling from the south. The English encountered no opposition on their march. Knowing that in previous campaigns the Scots had preferred not to fight, but instead to rely on raiding supply lines and ambushing patrols, some Englishmen may have been hoping that the expedition could be completed without any serious fighting at all. Such hopes were dashed in the late morning of 23 June when Scottish light cavalry were spotted drawn up astride the main road to Stirling on a hill at Gartclush.

The Scottish horsemen were led by Sir Alexander Keith and had been placed there by Robert Bruce to watch for the approach of the English army.

Robert Bruce had been keeping an eye on the English preparations, but was reluctant to face Edward in open battle. His experience in the war so far was that the English tended to win the set piece battles, while the Scots gained victory through ambush, raid and guerilla warfare. Bruce's intention was to mount a defence of the road to Stirling, but then to slip away rather than risk defeat. There would be plenty of time to come back and capture Stirling once the main English army had been forced to go back to England by lack of supplies.

Bruce left it to the last minute to muster his men, hoping thereby to save himself money and to ensure his men were fresh. By the time the army had gathered on the 21 June it seems to have comprised about 8,000 men. Of these about 500 were cavalry, mostly lightly equipped hobilars and only a few dozen knights. Around 6,000 of the infantry were armoured and properly equipped, while some 2,000 were Small Folk. The army was camped at Borestone Brae, where the modern visitor centre stands, but Bruce had decided to fight his delaying action on the banks of a stream just to the southeast, the Bannock Burn.

Just to the north of the Bannock Burn the road from Falkirk to Stirling crossed a stretch of open grassland, then rose up a short, steep slope to enter an area of woodland called The Park. Bruce knew that his main danger lay in the English heavy cavalry, so the flat land between the burn and The Park was turned into a trap. His men spent days digging pits that were designed to trip a horse and then covering them over with thin twigs and turf so that they could not be seen. The main defensive line was positioned just inside the trees where undergrowth and trees gave further protection against the English knights.

To the east of The Park was a large area of open grassland and boggy marsh around the lower reaches of the Bannock Burn. This was known as the Carse and was considered impassable for the wagons carrying the English supplies. Further north the Carse ended in woodland and low hills before it reached Stirling Castle.

Bruce took command of the force which was positioned on the edge of the Park, blocking the road to Stirling. The men commanded by Sir James Douglas were to his left. The main fighting was expected to take place here, but Bruce thought it wise to guard against an English flank attack over The Carse. The Earl of Moray was therefore positioned further back on the left to guard against such an attack. The position of Edward Bruce and his men at this point is unknown. The Small Folk (see page 17) were pushed back to the north of Coxet Hill where they would be out of the way.

Then the Scots waited for the inevitable attack.

Chapter 2
Commanders at Banockburn

The Scottish army was led by Robert the Bruce, but he had the support of some loyal and talented lieutenants whose ability and courage was to play a decisive role in the battle. The Scottish leadership was united, experienced and capable, despite Edward's best efforts to lure Scottish nobles away from their allegiance.

Robert the Bruce was 40 years old and the veteran of numerous campaigns against the English. As a young man, Bruce fought alongside William Wallace, but in 1302 he made his peace with Edward I of England. His father died in 1304, so Bruce inherited not only his family estates and titles but also a claim to be King of Scotland. In early 1306 Bruce laid claim to the throne and was crowned king at Scone on 25 March. That move plunged him into constant war against England. He fought pitched battles and guerilla campaigns with equal skill. By the time of Bannockburn, Bruce was experienced, skilled and respected.

Thomas Randolph, Earl of Moray, is usually described as being Bruce's nephew though it is not entirely certain how the two men were related. His relationship with Bruce had been fraught. He backed Bruce in 1306, but was captured at Methven and changed sides to support Edward I. He was captured again in 1308 and brought before the Bruce. Instead of asking pardon, Moray stood proudly and denounced Bruce as a coward for engaging in guerilla warfare rather than facing the English in open battle. Bruce had him thrown into a dungeon.

It was not long before Moray had changed sides again and this time he would remain loyal to his uncle. On 14 March 1314 he led a daring attack on Edinburgh Castle. The castle stood atop an apparently impregnable rock, but Moray learned of a narrow path to the top. In the middle of the night he led a band of men up the path, surprised the English garrison and captured the castle. In the run up to Bannockburn, Bruce put Moray in charge of the vanguard of the Scottish army, a position of great responsibility.

Statue of King Robert the Bruce in front of Marischal College, Aberdeen. Robert was popular, competent and charismatic. The contrast with his English opponent at Bannockburn could not have been clearer.

Edward Bruce, Earl of Carrick and Robert's younger brother, commanded the central division of the Scottish army at Bannockburn. He was aged about 35 at the time, his date of birth has not been preserved, and like his brother he was a seasoned military commander. From 1306 onwards he was a loyal lieutenant to his brother, playing a leading role in the guerrilla warfare of those years. His greatest feat came in 1313 when he managed to capture Rutherglen Castle from the English. The castle had defied three attacks by Robert Bruce and was famed for its walls that were 5 feet thick and made of solid stone. It was Edward who made the deal with Mowbray, the English governor of Stirling Castle, that led to the Battle of Bannockburn, one of the few ill judged military moves he had made to date.

The fourth division of the Scottish army was officially commanded by Walter the Steward, but in reality was led by Sir James Douglas. Walter was the hereditary High Steward of Scotland, an exalted position that made him the king's representative whenever the king himself was absent. Walter was, however, barely in his teens so Bruce ensured that he had Douglas to keep an eye on things.

Sir James Douglas was widely known as Black Douglas due to his mass of unruly black hair and murderous nature. He was 29 or 30 at the time of the battle and a highly experienced commander. In 1304 he had sought an accommodation with Edward I of England, but Edward rebuffed him due to the fact that Douglas's father, Sir William Douglas, had been the first Scottish knight to back William Wallace. When Robert Bruce claimed the crown in 1306, Douglas hurried to join him and remained loyal ever after.

Douglas fought at the Battle of Methven, thereafter taking to guerrilla warfare with skill and passion. His most notorious incident came on Palm Sunday 1307 when he attacked the English garrison of Douglas Castle while they were in church. Dozens were killed in the church, the rest dragged outside to have their heads hacked off. On 19 February 1314 Douglas captured Roxburgh Castle, one of the strongest in Scotland, by a ruse. He had his men dress up as cattle, then move slowly towards the walls after nightfall. Once at the foot of the walls, the men dropped their disguises, threw up ladders and were over the walls in seconds. The garrison was slaughtered and the castle burned. Douglas then received the summons from Bruce to come to Stirling, arriving in time to take part in the Battle of Bannockburn.

The English army was led in person by King Edward II, one of the most unpopular of medieval English kings. He had endless arguments with his nobles, churchmen and Parliament. His subjects accused him of being lazy, incompetent, indecisive, spiteful and vindictive. There is little doubt that Edward was all these things, but the disasters that struck England during his reign were not all his fault.

A series of bad harvests led to famines among the people, and to a fall in tax revenues. Combined with the fact that Edward inherited serious debts from his father, King Edward I, the fall in revenues produced a crisis in government finances. Edward had recourse to raising new taxes, increasing existing ones and borrowing from Italian bankers, but he failed to solve the underlying problems and lurched from one crisis to the next.

11

Other kings had suffered similar problems, but Edward's predicament was made worse by his personality. He would much rather be listening to music, patronising artists or attending parties with his friends than attending to affairs of state. Senior noblemen or clergy who needed to talk to Edward about an important matter found themselves fobbed off time and again. Even worse, Edward relied on other people to do much of his work for him. Decisions were made by clerks and lowly staff, which did not go down well with the nobles expected to abide by those decisions. One such man came to be the focus of the frustrations and hostility of the nobles: Piers Gaveston.

Gaveston was a young knight from Gascony, a part of France then owned by the English monarchy, who had little to recommend him other than a handsome face, witty tongue and quick mind. Edward was enraptued by Gaveston and quickly delegated to him many government decisions and loaded him with honours and wealth. This naturally enraged the nobles, and Gaveston made things worse by teasing them and mocking their appearances with jokes, songs and nicknames.

The tomb of Sir James Douglas. After his death fighting the Moslems while on Crusade in Spain, Douglas's bones were packed into a casket and carried back to Scotland by Sir William Keith of Galston, who had missed the fatal battle due to an earlier injury. They were deposited in this tomb in St Bride's Kirk in Douglas, Lanarkshire, the seat of the Douglas family.

Increasingly, Edward and Gaveston formed a partnership that excluded others. They partied while England teetered on the edge of bankruptcy. After numerous disputes that came dangerously close to civil war, the nobles led by Thomas, Earl of Lancaster, had Gaveston exiled and Edward was forced to take the advice of a committee of barons. Two years later, in 1312, Edward disbanded the committee of nobles and Gaveston returned to England. Edward summoned his army to help him subdue the barons, but nobody responded. Lancaster, with the Earls of Warenne and Warwick, captured Gaveston, then had him murdered. Edward was furious and humiliated. He once again accepted the committee of nobles, but secretly began plotting his revenge on the nobles who murdered Gaveston.

It was at this inauspicious moment that Edward heard of events in Stirling. Edward knew he had to march into Scotland to save Stirling, but he also knew that hardly anyone in his own kingdom liked or respected him. When he summoned his nobles for war, many of them refused to turn up. The campaign leading up to Bannockburn would be marked by bickering between Edward and the nobles, and between the nobles themselves. A key problem was Edward's lack of active military experience. He had ridden alongside his father on campaign several times, but had never been given an independent command. It seems that nobody in the army trusted Edward's military judgement and so his orders were constantly questioned and disputed by men with more experience. Edward was aged 30 at the time of Bannockburn.

One of those who questioned the king's judgement was Aymer de Valance, Earl of Pembroke. Aged 40 in 1314, Pembroke was the veteran of numerous wars. He had fought against France in 1297, being noted for his valour and his calm decision making in battle. He defeated Robert the Bruce at the Battle of Methven in 1306, though he was then defeated by Bruce at Loudoun Hill the following year. Nevertheless he had experience of fighting in Scotland and was respected by the army. He was also trusted by Edward since he had played no part in the murder of Gaveston.

Humphrey Bohn, Earl of Hereford, was 38 years old at Bannockburn. As a young man he had fought in Scotland for several years as a junior commander to Edward I. His record was one of almost unbroken success, and he was certainly highly skilled at the less exciting - but necessary - military skills of finding good camping grounds and keeping the army well fed. It was these skills that led Edward I to make Hereford the Constable of England - in modern terms the army's Chief of Staff. However, Hereford was partly responsible for the murder of Gaveston, so Edward stripped him of this job. Instead Hereford was given the deliberately demeaning task of organising a group of infantrymen for the campaign.

The job of Constable was given to Gilbert Clare, Earl of Gloucester. Young, he was only 23, handsome and dashing Gloucester was a favourite of Edward II. He had campaigned in Scotland in 1308, but without much success and many people blamed him for allowing Robert Bruce to regain the initiative in the on-going war. Unsurprisingly his relations with Hereford were dreadful and the two men bickered endlessly on the march north.

Although only marginally involved in the battle, Sir Philip Mowbray was a key figure. Mowbray was the son of English knight Sir Geoffrey Mowbray and Eve, daughter of John Comyn, Lord of Badenoch. He was therefore the grandson of the Red Comyn whom Bruce had murdered in 1306. On account of both parents, Mowbray was unlikely to support Robert the Bruce and indeed he sided with the English. Mowbray was made Governor of Stirling Castle in 1312 and still held that position when Edward Bruce laid siege to the castle in the spring of 1314. It was Mowbray who suggested to Edward Bruce that the siege should be relaxed on condition that he would surrender if not relieved by 24 June. The deal precipitated the Battle of Bannockburn.

Among the more junior noblemen, two would play a key role in the battle. The first of these was Robert Clifford, Lord Skipton, from Yorkshire. Clifford was aged about 40 and had spent much of his life on campaign. He was a younger son of a minor nobleman from Herefordshire and so would normally not expect to inherit. However, his mother's sister left him some lands which he used as a base for a career of acquisitiveness that by 1314 had made him a wealthy man as well as a respected soldier. Clifford was a favoured commander of Edward I, who gave him numerous military tasks and rich rewards for success. When Edward I died, Clifford was appointed to be an advisor to the new king. Edward II did not appreciate being nagged by older men who had been friends of his father, so Clifford was quickly dismissed. He retired to his estates, but rallied to Edward for the invasion of Scotland. Perhaps he saw the campaign as a chance to get himself back into his monarch's good books.

Another important figure at Bannockburn would be Henry Beaumont, Earl of Buchan. Beaumont chose to side with Edward I when Robert Bruce declared himself King of Scotland in 1306, and so was deprived of his earldom by the new king though he continued to use the title declaring that since he did not recognise

Bruce as King of Scotland, he did not recognise the forfeiture of his title. Beaumont was, in fact, no Scot but had gained his title by marriage. His background was as a younger son of the Vicomte de Beaumont in Maine who sought to gain fame and fortune by joining the court of King Edward I. He is known to have fought alongside Edward at the Battle of Falkirk in 1298 and was active in the Scottish wars until Edward's death. In 1310 Edward II ordered him to leave court in disgrace for some unknown reason, but he was back by the autumn of 1311 and seems to have been on friendly terms with the English king in 1314.

King Edward II of England was one of the most unpopular kings ever to rule England, a fact that helped cause his defeat at Bannockburn.

Chapter 3
Men, Weapons and Tactics

The armies of Scotland at this date were unique in Europe. There was nothing quite like them for they drew on both Scottish culture and on Scottish experience to create an army that was unusual in the way it was raised, its composition and its tactics.

For the detail of Scottish military arrangements in 1314 we rely on a number of documents dating to about this time. If none of them tell us exactly what happened in the year of Bannockburn, they do explain what was usual at the time. For instance, in 1318 King Robert the Bruce issued a Statute of Arms which told every local official exactly what he was expected to do in times of war. The Statute makes it clear that this is merely a slight updating of customary practice, so we can assume that what was true in 1318 was pretty much true in 1314.

Under the Statute of Arms it was the local thane, or royal official, who was responsible for ensuring that a powerful armed force was

A Scottish infantryman from the early 14th century as described in the contemporary Statue of Arms. He carries as his main weapon a spear that was specified to be a minimum of 12 feet long, though some men carried weapons 14 feet long. His small shield is of boiled leather with a metal boss covering the handgrip. Wielding the long Scottish spear was a two-handed job so a larger shield would have been impracticable. The helmet is made of iron, padded with wool. This man wears no other armour, though rather wealthier men would have had an aketon or perhaps even a mail shirt. The tunic may be of linen or wool, but the long cloak was invariably of wool and usually brightly patterned. The legs were usually bare and some men went barefoot, though others had leather boots.

16

ready to serve the king in time of war. To make sure that all was ready he had to summon a "wappinschaw" (weapon showing) every year in the week after Easter. At the wappinschaw every man liable for military service had to parade at a specified place so that the thane could inspect their equipment and themselves.

There were two main elements to the Scottish army at this date. The older and larger element was made up of the Common Army. This Common Army was composed of every able-bodied freeman (slaves and serfs were excluded) who was expected to turn out to fight for the king whenever he was told to do so. Each man was given 8 days to muster for war and was instructed to bring "sufficient" food so that he did not steal food from the countryside during campaign.

There were three classes of men in the Common Army. At the bottom of the social scale were men who were so poor that they did not own any livestock at all, not even a milk cow. These men were expected to turn up unarmed and unarmoured, presumably they would undertake menial duties such as digging latrines and the like. Some no doubt carried agricultural tools that could be used as weapons - knives, axes and the like - but they did not have specifically military weapons. These men were generally termed "the small folk" and were not expected to fight in a battle.

The middle ranking men in the Common Army were those who could afford livestock, but whose total possessions were valued at less than £10. These men had to appear armed to fight in a battle. Each man was expected to come with either a bow or a spear and shield. It would appear that most of these men also wore a helmet, but that very few of them had body armour of any kind.

Mention of a bow in the Statute ties in with several other contemporary references to the Scottish rulers seeking to increase the number of archers in their armies. In general the efforts were in vain, for only the men of Ettrick Forest are mentioned as having consistently come armed with bows in sufficient numbers. Lack of bowmen would cost Scottish armies dearly in some campaigns.

Those with goods worth more than £10 had to come with spear, shield, helmet, gauntlets and a type of body armour known as an "aketon". The aketon was a long-sleeved jacket that reached down to the knees and buttoned up the front all the way to the neck, with a stand up collar around the neck. It was made of a thick, closely woven fabric made of linen or wool, which was quilted together as many as 20 or 30 layers thick. The better quality examples had each piece of fabric cut to shape, the cheaper ones had odd shaped bits and pieces for the inner layers.

A diagram showing how a Scottish schiltron was deployed in the field. The core of the schiltron, and its best known component, was a densely formed block of infantry armed with long spears. These men formed up in a roughly oval or sometimes square formation. The solid front of men with shields and spears held out horizontally in action, vertically for marching, was proof against cavalry and as it lacked flanks or rear did not offer such vulnerable features to enemy attack. Scottish medieval armies were usually short on archers and mounted knights. The archers that were present would be pushed forward in a loose formation to shoot at the enemy, but would retreat within the schiltron when threatened. The knights or light cavalry would be held back behind the schiltron, perhaps 300 yards behind, to await the opportunity to charge at a crumbling enemy formation or to come forward if needed to cover the retreat of the schiltron.

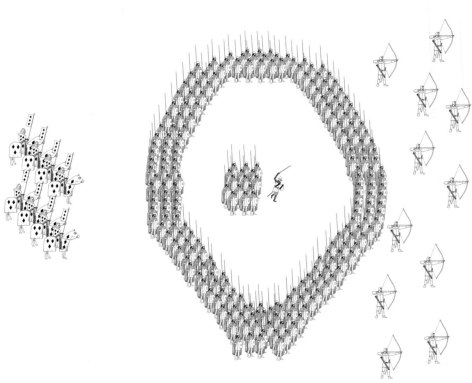

Armour made or linen may not sound very effective, but the aketon was a surprisingly useful piece of kit. It could withstand blows from most types of weapon, while the padding absorbed the force of the impact and spread the incoming energy across a wide area so as to minimise bruising. Against slashing blows, or light weapons the aketon was proof, but it was vulnerable to a thrust from a very sharp weapon, or to a heavy blow from a polearm. Another Statute of Arms from a couple of generations later stipulated that richer freemen had to have a coat of mail or scale armour, presumably as the aketeon had by then proved to be less than ideal, though still serviceable.

The sufficient food that these men were expected to bring along is not specified in the Statute, but is mentioned in contemporary chronicles. Each man had with him a sack of oatmeal and a broad, flat stone. Each evening some of the oatmeal was mixed with water into a thick paste and then spread on the stone in front of a fire to cook into a tough, hard biscuit. These biscuits formed the basis of the evening meal, along with any cheese, fish, meat or vegetables that could be found locally. Left over biscuit was carried in a pouch to be nibbled on during the following day.

Every man was also expected to bring with him a mount of some kind. Richer men had ponies, the poorer ones mules or donkeys. The mount carried the man, his equipment and his food. At the end of each day's march the ponies were hobbled, then turned out to graze on whatever vegetation they could find. A Flemish chronicler was aghast at the poor fodder that the Scottish ponies ate with apparent relish. Whereas war horses from his own country would expect lush grass and grain, the Scottish ponies browsed heather and bushes.

The fact that every man was mounted gave the Scottish Common Army a marching speed far in excess of the English army, which marched primarily on foot. While the English reckoned 12 to 14 miles was a good day's travel, the Scots regularly made 25 miles a day and sometimes more. Not only did this mean that a Scottish army could out run or catch up with an English army, it also allowed a Scottish commander to keep his units dispersed over a wide area, and then suddenly bring them together to form a large army where the English thought there was none.

In terms of their equipment the men of the Common Army were not markedly inferior to many other soldiers in Europe at this date. Where they seem to have been deficient in most circumstances was in terms of training. There was no stipulation in the Statute of Arms that these men had to practice with their weapons or take part in drills. So long as they had the correct equipment, that was thought good enough. Compared to many other armies active in Europe at the time, including the English army, this put the Scots Common Army at a distinct disadvantage.

The second element of the Scottish army was the Feudal Host. Feudalism had been introduced to Scotland over a prolonged period of time by several kings, but even by 1308 it affected only parts of the kingdom and nowhere was it comprehensive.

The basis of feudalism was that the king exchanged land for military service in a society where cash and money were little used. The king gave to a man the right to draw the rents and other income from a parcel of land. In return that man had to give military service to the king. In peacetime the military service would take the form of garrisoning castles, patrolling the border or providing muscle to help royal officials with their duties - such as collecting taxes. Generally each man was expected to serve for 40 days, but very often he was required for longer and would be paid in cash or kind for the additional days.

As elsewhere the basic unit of feudal landholding was the "fee". This was the amount of land that produced enough income to provide an adequate income for a knight. The money freed the knight from the need to work, allowing him to spend all his time training for war. It also provided enough money to purchase and maintain a war horse, riding horse, armour and weapons as well as pay for a squire and attendants. In Scotland many of the fees were subdivided into half fees, quarter fees or even smaller. These smaller parcels of land were intended to provide enough income to maintain, not a knight but an armoured infantry man, light cavalryman or other useful military soldier. On the West Coast this feudal system took a unique form as the smaller fee divisions provided men for the Scottish navy.

A key advantage of the feudal system from the point of Scottish monarchs is that it provided a large number of well-equipped, fully trained men who had no business other than fighting or training for war. There were fewer of these men than could be raised from the same land by means of the Common Army, but the men were far more effective on campaign and in battle.

It is difficult to be certain due to records having been lost, but by about 1300 it is likely that about a quarter to a third of the Scottish military effort came from the feudal host, the rest from the Common Army. On individual campaigns that ratio may have fluctuated somewhat but was probably fairly standard.

The Scots had, by this date, developed a unique tactical deployment that would serve them well in some circumstances, but not in others: the schiltron. The core of the schiltron was the mass of men armed with long spears and small shields that made up the bulk of both the Common Army and infantry raised by feudal means. These men formed up in a hollow circle, oval or square with the outside composed of between three and six ranks of men. The men stood shoulder to shoulder and in action held their spears horizontally in front of them to present a hedge of wickedly sharp spikes to the enemy.

The formation was based on the older shield wall, used right across northern Europe, which had faced forward to the enemy. The schiltron was a reaction against the heavy cavalry made up of armoured knights which could smash the flanks or rear of a shield wall and reduce an army to a fleeing mob of fugitives to be cut down at will. Because a schiltron had neither flanks nor rear, it could not be broken in this way.

At the centre of the schiltron stood the knight or nobleman who commanded it, together with a small body of spearmen who could be used to plug any gaps in the outer line that threatened to appear. Such archers as were to hand were usually

This figure shows the type of armour that was typical of the majority of knights and esquires in the both the English and Scottish armies. He has a suit of chain mail that totally encases his body, with mail gauntlets and mail boots protecting even his feet and hands. His coat of arms is repeated on his shield, surcout and horse's camparison. The squared flag on his lance marks him as a knight banneret, a senior rank of knight that ceased to be used in the later medieval period. His helmet is of iron, padded inside with leather and wool and has been shaped to deflect blows from enemy weapons

pushed forward ahead of the schiltron. There they would shoot at the enemy, seeking to break up their formations before battle was joined. Cavalry were held back behind the schiltron to be deployed when needed. Heavy cavalry would charge at any gaps in the enemy formation to smash it open and break it up. Lighter cavalry would be used to pursue an already broken enemy.

In the event of defeat, the horsemen should fight a rearguard action to give the infantry time to get away. This did not always happen as the men on horses were as keen to escape a disaster as anyone else, so the infantry sometimes eyed their own cavalry warily.

The English military system was far more feudalised than the Scottish. It is thought that by about 1300 England contained around 8,000 "fees". Each fee was expected to produce a knight, who brought with him one man at arms and four or so infantry. Some fees were subdivided, as in Scotland, to produce infantry or light horsemen. The King of England had many demands on his military manpower, since he had to garrison a large number of castles and coastal defences on a permanent basis, so many of the military men would have served out their feudal duty close to home and not been available for campaigns.

The monarch did, however, have other ways to raise an army. Towns and counties were obliged to answer a Commission of Array. The commission of array for a town instructed the local officials to find a

This man's equipment is the ideal to which the English infantry that fought at Bannockburn would aspire, though many would fail to have the full kit. His helmet is of iron, padded inside with a thick leather lining stuffed with wool. The mail hauberk has a coif under the helmet and reaches to the thighs and elbows. Over the hauberk he wears a sleeveless tunic made of thick leather on to which have been sewn overlapping scales made from horn. His triangular shield is about 30 inches tall and 24 inches wide and is made of thin, overlapping sheets of wood faced with boiled leather. His main weapon is a 10 foot long thrusting spear, with a short sword for back up.

set number of volunteers, and to persuade those men who would be staying at home to pay the money to equip those who were going. There was no set number that a town was expected to produce and each time the commissions were issued the numbers varied depending on how many men the king wanted in his army.

There were also, of course, a number of non-combatants that went on campaign. The most numerous of these were the government officials who had to go everywhere the king went. In addition, the royal kitchen was expected to feed any barons or senior knights who happened to be near the king at dinner time. For the king not to invite such men to dine with him would have been a serious breach of chivalrous protocol. There were also a number of military specialists in the direct pay of the king. On one campaign a few years later, these included 12 blacksmiths, 40 carpenters and 60 miners. There were also friars and priests who ministered to the spiritual needs of the army along with doctors to care for men who fell ill as well as for the wounded.

The basic infantry tactic was the shield wall. This was composed of several ranks of men, usually 8 or so deep, standing shoulder to shoulder. They presented their overlapping shields to the enemy to form a solid wall of shields - hence the name of the formation. Good men could move about the battlefield at a jog and still maintain formation, though most preferred to walk and even then might have to stop every now and then to get back into shape.

Most infantrymen came armed with a spear, which was used to stab at the enemy over the top of a shield wall, but others came to war with axes, swords or bows. There seems to have been little effort made to separate out these men. They all formed up in the shield wall as a mixed mass of different weaponry, presumably with all the men from one area choosing to stand together.

The basic cavalry tactic was the charge, delivered by two or three ranks of horsemen riding knee to knee. Each rank was 20 or so yards behind the one in front so that if a horse fell those behind stood a chance of jumping over it or veering out the way before they too were brought down. A charge of armoured knights delivered at the right time was devastating. Choosing when to launch this charge was perhaps the most important decision a 13th century commander had to make. Well formed infantry could withstand a charge for no horse will gallop straight into a solid object - including a wall of men. But even the slightest disorder would cause a formation to crack under the impact of a charge. Poorly trained infantry would often simply run away in the face of a charge of knights.

And once an army was fragmented and fleeing a commander would find it very difficult indeed to restore order and discipline.

Chapter 4
The Battle of Bannockburn
The First Day

Edward II of England learned of the Scottish position on the far bank of the Bannock Burn late on the morning of 23 June. It was a hot day and the men were already tired from marching for hours in full armour. They were no doubt grateful of the chance for a sit down and a rest while Edward called a council of war to consult with his commanders.

The English ambition was not so much to defeat Bruce as to get through to Stirling Castle and so achieve a relief under the terms of the agreement. Defeating Bruce could be left to another day. It was decided that a large scale attack would drive directly up the road over the Bannock Burn and into The Park. This force of both cavalry and infantry would be led by the Earl of Hereford and the Earl of Gloucester. Meanwhile a smaller force of about 500 cavalry would move across the Carse commanded by Clifford and Beaumont. It was hoped that this threat to their flank would cause the Scots in The Park to retreat and so open the way to Stirling Castle. If not, perhaps the horsemen could ride right around the Scottish army to reach Stirling and so effect the formal relief on their own.

The battle began at about noon with the advance of Hereford and Gloucester getting under way. The force first had to get over the Bannock Burn, then deploy to attack. While the English were coming down the steep hill to funnel over the burn and then get into formation to attack across the flat land beyond, Robert Bruce rode out of the woods to ride up and down in front of his army. It is presumed that he did so to shout words of encouragement to his men. Whatever the reason, Bruce clearly did not expect the fighting to start any time soon. He was not mounted on his war horse but on his garron, a type of hardy but lightweight riding horse, nor was he in full armour.

Seeing the Scottish king in a vulnerable position an English knight named Sir Henry de Bohun spurred forwards. Bohun was the young nephew of the Earl of

Hereford and no doubt eager to earn fame, glory and rewards by taking on a king in single combat. If Bruce were to be killed or captured the war might be over, with England as the victor. Even if Bohun was driven off, he would have become famous. Famous he was to become, but for the wrong reasons.

Bruce saw Bohun coming and at once appreciated his danger. However, the King of Scots could not flee from single combat at the start of a battle. The blow to morale of the Scottish army would be too great to contemplate. Bruce was himself a fully trained knight who would normally go into battle armed and equipped as was Bohun and similarly riding a big warhorse. Bruce knew that a charge by heavily armoured, mounted knights could be devastating, but he was also aware of the limitations of a lone knight. Bruce sat patiently on his riding horse as the lumbering Bohun thundered down at him. The only sign that Bruce was aware of his danger came when he lifted his battleaxe to his shoulder.

Right at the last moment, as Bohun's levelled lance was seemingly about to strike the Scottish king in his chest, Bruce edged his horse suddenly sideways a crucial few inches, then span around and struck with his battleaxe. The blow hit Bohun on the top of the helmet, smashed its way through the metal and buried itself deep in the man's skull, killing him instantly. For a few seconds Bohun's lifeless body remained upright in the saddle as his warhorse continued its charge, but then it slowly toppled to one side and collapsed to the ground. The Scots army cheered.

The first blow to be struck at the Battle of Bannockburn was struck by King Robert Bruce himself when he was attacked by the English knight Henry de Bohun. Bruce famously killed the English knight with a single blow of his battle axe.

Bruce rode back to the ranks to be surrounded by cheering men congratulating him on his feat. But all Bruce could say was that he had just broken his best axe and where was he going to get another one as good?

Meanwhile the rest of the English force had shaken itself into formation and moved forward. Exactly what happened is not entirely clear as none of the chroniclers gives a detailed account. What is known is that the force going forwards was made up of infantry, archers and cavalry. The conventional approach that most commanders would have used would be for the infantry to advance in a solid block, presenting a wall of shields toward the enemy. Mixed in with the infantry would be archers, mostly in the rear ranks. The heavily armoured knights would be riding behind or on the flanks of the infantry phalanx.

Ordinarily the archers would start to shoot as soon as they got within range. Their arrows would inflict casualties on the enemy, weakening their force and, it was hoped, opening up gaps in the enemy formation. If those gaps proved to be great enough, or if the commander judged the enemy to be vulnerable in some way, the knights would charge. A mass of charging knights could smash a formation apart, but was usually unleashed only when it was reasonably certain that they could triumph. If the enemy force appeared too solid for the charge to have much chance of success, the infantry phalanx would close to hand-to-hand combat to inflict casualties and so open the way for a charge.

But Hereford and Gloucester would have seen at once that there was a problem. The Scots had positioned themselves just inside the line of trees. Arrows would be ineffective as they would most likely get caught or deflected by the tree branches. Moreover, the undergrowth in The Park would make it difficult for the horsemen to charge riding stirrup to stirrup as they would normally do. Bruce had positioned his men well.

From the fragmentary comments that have survived, it seems that Hereford and Gloucester advanced with their infantry leading the way and the knights riding behind. As the infantry approached The Park they had to climb a slope to get at the Scots. The English were beaten back, but seem to have performed a reasonably orderly retreat rather than collapsing in rout. The training in which the Englishmen who answered the Commission of Array took part was proving its worth.

As the infantry fell back the knights would have moved forward to deter the Scots from following up their success. Any Scotsman who sought to dash forward to cut off stragglers would quickly be cut down by the English horsemen. It was normal practice, but it was at this point that the Earl of Gloucester fell foul of one of the hidden pits dug by the Scots the day before. His horse fell, throwing the earl to the ground, then bolted. Gloucester was quickly on his feet and other horsemen hurried to his side to deter any Scottish attack, but even so Gloucester had to walk back to rejoin his men. It was a humiliation he would remember the following morning.

As the attack led by Gloucester and Hereford ran out of steam and was driven back, the column of horsemen led by Clifford and Beaumont was doing rather better. They had splashed their way over the lower Bannock Burn and were advancing across the Carse unhindered. Now free from dealing with Gloucester and Hereford, Bruce was able to pay attention to what was going on elsewhere. Alerted to the advance of the 500 horsemen, Bruce demanded to know what Moray was doing. On being told he was remaining under cover of the trees, Bruce sent a messenger to his nephew with a cryptic, if pointed message.

"I see that a rose has fallen from your chaplet", said Bruce.

Bruce was referring to the custom of presenting a man who had performed well in battle with a wreath made of whatever suitable plants were to be found on the battlefield. It was a way for a commander to acknowledge gallant conduct on the spot, and frequently led to later more valuable reward in the form of cash or kind. Whether or not Moray had recently been given a chaplet in recognition of his daring victory of capturing Edinburgh Castle we don't know, but he certainly got the point of Bruce's barbed remark.

Moray at once formed his men into a schiltron and marched them out of the trees to descend to the flat land of the Carse and block the English horsemen's advance on Stirling. As the Scots formation of perhaps 2,000 infantry emerged and moved east they were watched by Clifford and Beaumont. Riding beside the two leaders was a senior knight named Sir Thomas Grey of Heaton. Grey had crossed swords with William Wallace himself at Lanark in 1297 and been so badly wounded that the Scots had left him for dead. Grey had recovered and fought in several skirmishes in the years that followed before being captured by the Scots in 1303 and then escaping in dramatic fashion. He had fought alongside Beaumont at the siege of Stirling in 1304 and the two men seem to have got on well, which makes what happened next all the more baffling.

As the Scots deployed, Beaumont brought the column of horsemen to a halt and remarked "Let us wait here a while. Let them come on, let them come on out on to the plain".

The view across the Carse from the Bannock Burn looking north, the view that Beaumont and Clifford had as they began their march. The Pelstream Burn is marked by the trees in the middle distance, while the rounded hill beyond is Abbey Craig, topped by the 19th century Wallace Monument.

A few minutes later Grey pointed to the Scots and said "Sir, I fear there are too many of them."

"Look you!" snapped back Beaumont "If you are afraid then you can go back now."

Grey was understandably offended. He pushed his horse to be in front of Beaumont's and declared "Sir! It is not through fear that I shall go this afternoon." He edged his horse forward towards the Scots a short distance, then turned to stare at Beaumont as if challenging him to give the order to attack. It was a direct affront to Beaumont's dignity and right to command, and Beaumont must have realised that it was.

However, it was Clifford who took matters in hand. He spurred his horse forward to join Grey and waved his arm to give the order to attack. The armoured knight, esquires and men at arms surged forward. This was what they had trained for from childhood. The mounted charge in close order of armoured horsemen

...ad dominated the battlefields of Europe for centuries. When delivered properly
t was a battle-winning tactic. But the Scots had an answer to the knightly charge:
he schiltron.

The English knights surged forward. The Scots infantry saw them coming and
prepared to receive them. The schiltron came to a halt and the front rank of men
knelt down, planting the butts of their spears firmly into the ground so that they
sloped upward and outward. The other ranks held their spears horizontally
forwards. Together the spears presented a solid hedge of wickedly sharp steel
points to the English. Grey's horse was one of those to go down to the Scottish
spears. He was knocked senseless as he fell and was captured. Others rode around
the schiltron fruitlessly seeking a way in.

Unable to get into the schiltron, Clifford and Beaumont rallied their horsemen
and fell back a short distance. They halted on the Carse, somewhere near the
Pelstream Burn, a much smaller waterway than the Bannock Burn. There they
sat their horses glaring at Moray's schiltron. After a while Moray led his men
back into the Park and out of view.

At around 3pm or so Edward II called another council of war. This time there
was a new arrival, Sir Robert Mowbray the governor of Stirling Castle had
managed to slip out of his fortress and make his way to the English army.
Although we do not have a detailed account of what passed at the meeting, it may
have been Mowbray who reiterated that the main task of the English army was
to reach Stirling Castle and relieve it, not to fight the Scottish army. This,
combined with the continuing belief among the senior English commanders that
they would always win a pitched battle against the Scots, decided Edward. He
now had less than 48 hours to reach the castle, so he had to break through the
Scots somehow. The action fought by Clifford and Beaumont against Moray may
have been inconclusive, but Moray had gone and the way across the Carse was
now clear. Edward decided to march across the Carse to Stirling.

The orders were sent out and the main body of the English army turned aside
from the main road from Falkirk to Stirling. They took a route not too far removed
from that now covered by the A91 down to the Bannock Burn, crossing the stream
about where Pike Road does today and heading north across the Carse.

It proved to be slow going as the banks of the stream were steep and much of
the surrounding land was marshy. This slowed down the infantry, but presented
a real barrier to the horsemen. As for the supply carts they would have been in
real trouble. There is some evidence that they were left south of the Bannock

Burn with an armed guard to protect them against a sneak Scottish attack. Presumably the men took with them enough food for a day or two away from the supply wagons, but some sources say the English did not eat breakfast next day as they lacked food, so perhaps they did not.

In any case it took most of the afternoon for the English army to get over the Bannock Burn and on to the Carse. The final march to relieve Stirling Castle would have to wait until the next day. In choosing a camp ground, Edward II's main concern would have been to guard against the sort of sneak, night time attack

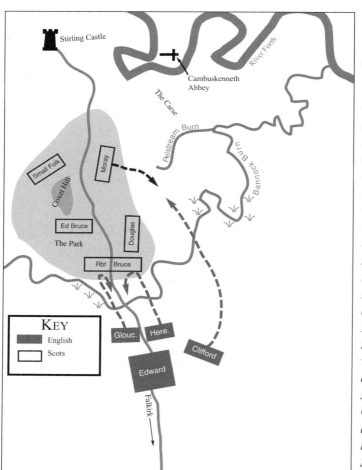

The Battle of Bannockburn began at about noon on 23 June when the English advancing from Falkirk sought to break through to Stirling Castle. The first attack was a combined infantry-cavalry assault launched straight up the main road by the Earl of Gloucester and the Earl of Hereford. A secondary move was a fast-moving cavalry column sent across the Carse. Both advances were blocked by the Scots.

at which Bruce and the Scots excelled. No large English army had ever been attacked by the Scots, but attempts to slit the throats of sentries or steal horses were real enough threats.

Edward therefore chose to pitch camp on the flat, dry land between the Bannock Burn and the Pelstream Burn. This meant that the English camp had water on three sides. Any Scots approaching at night would almost inevitably make splashing noises and so be heard by English sentries. And next day the English army could march out, turn right and make for Stirling across the flat Carse that was still temptingly clear of Scottish soldiers. The English soldiers did not like the spot, it was damp and exposed to the wind while the lack of trees meant they had no firewood to build fires to cook supper and warm themselves. The nobles were none to pleased either. Gloucester would seem to have wanted to press on to Stirling that evening, while Hereford was sniping at Edward for a lack of resolve. The old charges of indecision were again being levelled at the king.

One knight in the English camp, Sir Alexander Seton, had had enough. He was a lowland Scot and, like many of his type, had divided loyalties. He did not welcome Edward's overlordship, but neither did he support the Bruce's claim to the Scottish throne. As sun set over the dispirited English army and its bickering leadership, Seton seems to have made his mind up as to whose side he was on. He slipped away in the darkness and went in search of Bruce.

Seton found Bruce at the Scottish camp at the Borestone deep in the Park. A debate was going on amongs the Scottish high command, though it was free of the bad tempered squabbling taking place down on the Carse. Bruce was of the opinion that the Scottish army had performed well. Twice that day they had driven off an attack by the English in open battle. The Scots had chosen their defensive ground well, drawn up in good order and fought bravely. And they had beaten the King of England. True Edward II was despised by everyone who knew him and had a non-existent reputation for military prowess, but he was still an anointed king and that counted for a great deal in the medieval mind. Bruce believed that the Scottish army had done enough. It was time to melt away, allow Stirling Castle to be relieved and then wait for the English army to go home before coming back to lay siege again and continue the guerilla war.

Douglas and Moray disagreed. They had seen the English had fought badly and that their own men had done well. They wanted to stay and fight again for a second day, to inflict even more damage on the English army and English pride.

It was at this point that Seton was brought in by the Scottish pickets. He told Bruce about the dismal state of the English army.

"The English have lost heart," he said. "They are uncertain and are dreading a sudden assault."

Bruce was silent for a while then he suddenly stood up. "Now is the time," he declared. The next day was going to see more bloodshed.

The view from the English camping ground across the Carse to Stirling Castle. Only about two miles separated King Edward of England from his goal as the English army bedded down. Edward expected an easy march over the Carse to the castle the next morning.

Chapter 5
The Battle of Bannockburn
The Second Day

The Battle of Bannockburn's second day began while it was still dark. Neither Robert Bruce nor Edward II had anything to do with the opening moves, and it is unlikely that they knew much about them either.

David Strathbogie, Earl of Atholl, was a bitter enemy of Robert Bruce though the cause of the feud is not entirely clear. His father, also Earl of Atholl, had been executed by the English, while his sister was mistress to Edward Bruce. Nevertheless Atholl never missed a chance to seek to undermine Bruce's claim to the throne. When Bruce did become king, he took the opportunity to deprive Atholl of lands and so Atholl offered to help Edward II. Atholl was not marching with the English army, but was on the north side of the Forth mustering men from his estates. We do not know quite when he came down to Stirling, but no doubt he was attracted there by news of the English advance and may well have been co-ordinating his moves with Edward.

Atholl and his men were in the hills above Blairlogie from where they had a grandstand view of events. On 23 June they had watched the progress of the English army. More interestingly they had also seen the movements of Bruce's baggage train and supply wagons. They had been moved to the north bank of the Forth to be out of the reach of the English and were parked in the grounds of Cambuskenneth Abbey with only a small guard under sir John Airth. It was a tempting target, and Atholl decided to grab it.

At a little after midnight on 23 June Atholl and his men advanced warily toward Cambuskenneth. Atholl need not have worried for Airth was keeping a slack watch. The attack achieved complete surprise. Airth was killed, as were all his men who failed to run away in time. Atholl gleefully began a thorough and determined looting of Bruce's baggage, stealing everything of value. As dawn broke Atholl left for the hills, fearing that Bruce would come to take revenge.

33

The bell tower at Cambuskenneth Abbey. The second day of battle began here when the Earl of Atholl raided Bruce's baggage train that was parked in the abbey's grounds. In 1314 this was one of the most important abbeys in Scotland, enjoying royal patronage since its founding by David I in 1140 and benefitting from its proximity to the royal burgh and fortress of Stirling. It remained of key importance for centuries after the battle, with Bruce holding a parliament here in 1326. It was closed in 1559 during the Reformation and today only the bell tower remains intact.

In fact, Bruce had more important matters in hand. Dawn comes early in Scotland in June, around 3.30am. The Scottish army was woken up more than an hour before dawn and told to eat breakfast, then to arm and stand ready to march. Those who thought they would be marching north or west were in for a shock. They were to march east to attack the English.

Bruce drew his men up in six formations. On the right was Edward Bruce with his division drawn up in a schiltron. On Edward Bruce's left was Moray with his men similarly arranged. Behind these two formations and covering the small gap between them was Douglas with his infantry. Bruce himself was behind Douglas, holding his division in reserve so that he could deploy it where it was most needed as the battle unfolded. Alongside Bruce was Keith with the small number of Scottish cavalry. The Small Folk left their camp near Coxtet Hill and came up behind Bruce and Keith, though whether this was on their own initiative or because of orders from Bruce is unclear.

As the cold, grey light of the predawn spread over the Carse, the English army began to stir. There was no wood for fires, so those that had any food for breakfast had to eat it cold. Slowly the men began to get ready for the day's march to Stirling. Some thought there would be fighting to brush the Scots aside, others thought the Scots would have fled in the night.

Yet another argument began to rage inside the tent of Edward II. The Earls of Hereford and Gloucester, among the more experienced of the senior nobles in fighting the Scots, wanted to remain camped on the Carse for the day. He pointed out that the deadline to reach Stirling Castle was the following day, that the men were hungry and dispirited after the setback the previous day and that the supply

Before battle was joined the Scottish army knelt in prayer and Abbot Muireach, of Inchaffray followed the prayers by exhortations to the army to be faithful to old Scottish saints and fight well.

wagons were still south of the Bannock Burn. Edward's younger favourites, on the other hand, wanted to move at once. He had little time for the Scots, thinking that Bruce had merely been lucky the day before. As the argument grew more heated Edward mocked Gloucester for having been forced to walk back to the ranks the day before. Someone then brought up Gloucester's ambivalent role in the events leading up to Gaveston's death and declared he had never been loyal to Edward as king. Words such as "traitor" and "liar" were heard.

"God's Truth" raged Gloucester in his fury. "This day it will be clear that I am neither traitor nor liar." Then he stormed out of the royal tent. What Gloucester was expecting to see in the dim light of dawn we do not know. Certainly he did not expect to see the entire Scottish army marching in battle array out of the woodland on the Park - but that is what he saw.

Edward and the other nobles came out into the open to stare at Bruce's advancing schiltrons. The reactions of the men varied. Edward stood staring in

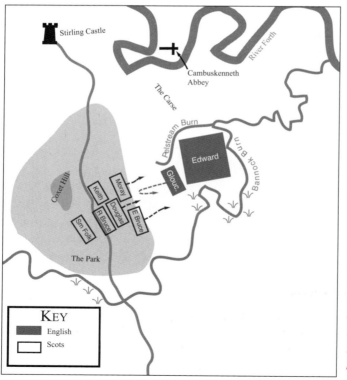

Soon after dawn on 24 June the reformed Scottish army advanced to attack the English army as it lay in camp. Moray and Edward Bruce led the advance with Douglas, while Robert Bruce kept the reserve under his own control. The Earl of Gloucester was the first man on the English side to react, leading a charge of heavily armoured cavalry that came to grief on the points of the Scottish spears.

disbelief at the Scots with his household knights by his side. Gloucester, however, reacted quickly. He has been accused by some of panicking, but almost certainly he saw the danger that the English army was now in. By camping on flat ground with water on three sides of them, the English had made themselves proof against nocturnal raids by the Scots. But now those same waters looked like becoming a trap. The English army would not be able to get across them, so there was only one way out - and Bruce's schiltrons were advancing to close that gap and trap the English.

Experienced commander that he was, Gloucester will have known that previous English successes had hinged upon having room for the better trained English soldiers to manoeuver, but the camping ground chosen by Edward II was barely half a square mile in extent and the men were jammed closely together. They

A Victorian view of dawn on the day of battle. Robert Bruce points toward the English army as he addresses his troops and explains his plan of battle to them. The picture has a number of inconsistencies regarding equipment, but well captures the eagerness of the Scottish army to get to grips with the invaders.

would have no room to manoeuver and their main tactical advantages over the Scots would be lost.

Something had to be done, and Gloucester knew only too well that indecisive, inexperienced Edward II was not the man to do it. Gloucester raced over to his own men, shouting orders for them to get armed and mounted. Hereford, meanwhile, seems to have concentrated on getting the infantry into formation - though as with so much about the English in this battle it is difficult to be certain.

Edward, meanwhile, was still standing watching the Scots advance. Once the Scots were out of the woodland they halted, dressed their lines and then knelt down.

"See, they kneel. They kneel," smirked Edward. "They beg for mercy."

Beside him stood the grizzled old warrior Sir Ingelram Umfraville, who had been fighting the Scots for over 20 years. He stared at his king in contempt.

"Oh yes, sire," he scornfully replied. "They beg for mercy, but not from you. Those men have come here to conquer or to die."

As if in answer to Umfraville's words the figure of a cleric emerged from the Scottish host and held up a cross. It was Muireach, Abbot of Inchaffray Abbey.

"Be it so," muttered Edward. "We will see."

Abbot Muireach was giving a rousing speech about the benefits of having the support of Scottish saints in the coming battle. He held up the silver reliquary that held the sacred armbone of St Fillan, an especially holy Irish monk who had come to Scotland and founded Inchaffray Abbey in the 8th Century. According to a later story, Muireach had left the sacred arm bone behind rather than risk it in battle and was waving only the empty box. Bruce insisted on opening the box to see the sacred relic before battle was joined, and when the reliquary lid was lifted the bone was there. Muireach later claimed this as a miracle.

Miracle or not, the Scots army finished their prayers, stood up and began to advance. They were met by a charge of mounted knights led by the Earl of Gloucester. His aim was to hold back the schiltrons long enough for the English army to deploy out of the trap into which their king had led them. Once deployed on the open ground of the Carse, the English would have the advantage.

Gloucester had got his men going in a hurry. They were not properly drawn up, nor did they all have full suits of armour on. Gloucester himself was fully armoured, but had not put on his surcoat that was embroidered with his coat of arms. How many times Gloucester charged we do not know. We do know that in one charge his horse was disemboweled by a Scottish spear and the earl rolled to the ground. Lacking the surcoat that marked him out as an earl worth a high ransom the Scots took him to be a mere man at arms and hacked him to death.

With Gloucester gone the English army lacked all leadership. There was no lack of courage or bravery, but with nobody directing the fighting the English army behaved more like a mob than an army. What King Edward was doing as Gloucester died we do not know. The contemporary accounts of the battle make no mention of his actions nor of any orders he may have given. He seems to have been an invisible man, so presumably he did nothing - or at least nothing useful.

Before long Bruce and his advancing schiltrons had closed the door on the English army, blocking the gap between the Pelstream Burn and Bannock Burn. The English armoured infantry were in formation by this point, but the narrow frontage meant that they could not deploy their greater numbers to get on to the flanks of the Scots. Nor could the armoured cavalry charge for their was no space for them to deploy and no open ground over which they could build up the speed

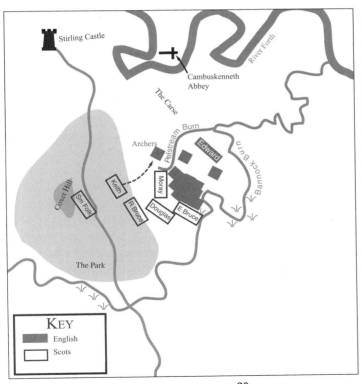

The Scottish advance was rapid, the schiltrons sealing the gap between the Pelstream Burn and Bannock Burn before the English could escape the trap. The advance of the Scottish spearmen, pushing steadily forward was relentless. A group of English archers sought to turn the tide, but they ridden down by Keith's cavalry.

necessary for their impact to be overwhelming. Every advantage that the English usually enjoyed was gone. And in the cramped space the long Scottish spears were showing themselves to be superior to the shorter English pole weapons.

For more than an hour the battle swayed back and forth as the masses of armoured infantry hacked at each other along the narrow frontage between the Bannock Burn and the Pelstream Burn.

Then someone on the English side led a group of archers over the Pelstream. Archers at this date wore no armour and so could wade across the stream and scramble up the far bank with ease. The archers strung their bows, then began to pour a murderous rain of arrows into the flank of Douglas's schiltron. With little in the way of armour the Scottish infantry died in their dozens. There was little that Douglas could do. Crossing the Pelstream would involve breaking the formation of his schiltron, and that would leave his men horribly vulnerable to any English cavalry that could get at them. Scottish casualties began to mount and some English infantry began working their way along the Peltstream Burn, threatening to get around the flank of Douglas and get into open ground where they could deploy properly.

Bruce was equal to the threat. He sent Keith's horsemen forward to sweep around Douglas's flank and crash into the lightly armed archers. The archers were swept away and Douglas rallied his men. Advancing again Douglas resealed the trap. There could now be no escape for the English.

Edward II was watching all this unfold around him as he sat his horse well to the rear of the English army. Beside was Sir Giles of Argentine, a Norman knight who had fought in the Crusades. He was in command of the handful of knights who formed Edward's bodyguard. Pembroke came back, battered and dazed, from the fighting line. He told Edward that the Scots were winning. Edward just stared, apparently unable to comprehend what was happening nor to make any decision. Pembroke turned to Argentine, who looked out over the confused and rapidly deteriorating situation. It was at this point that the Small Folk emerged from the trees of the Park. They were too far away for the English to see them clearly and were taken for a large body of well armed reinforcements. Pembroke and Argentine grabbed Edward's bridle and tugged the unprotesting monarch toward the Pelstream Burn.

The small knot of mounted knights splashed over the stream and slithered up the far side. As the brightly decorated royal banner moved off it was seen by some Scots horsemen, who gave chase. Argentine saw them and turned to Edward.

"Sire, I was placed in charge of your rein," he told the apparently dazed monarch. "There is your castle of Stirling where your body will be safe. For myself, I am not used to running away, nor shall I do so now. I commend you to God." With that he turned and spurred toward the pursuing Scots. He fought with his customary skill and held the Scots long enough for Pembroke to drag Edward away to safety, but Argentine could not win and he was eventually cut down.

The English had also seen Edward flee. The sight of their monarch running away was too much. The English army fragmented and broke as each man tried to flee the deadly Scottish spears advancing relentlessly on them. But the trap into which Edward had led them was deadly. Both the Bannock Burn and the Pelstream Burn were easy enough for a lone man to wade across, but as thousands of men tried to race across they became deadly. The streambeds were of thick mud that gripped the legs of the men, and pulled down their heavily armoured bodies. The steep banks were difficult to climb for men in armour, and those that made it up churned the banks to slippery mud making them increasingly difficult for those who followed to scale.

With all discipline gone and formation lost, the English army quickly became a fleeing mob. And still the relentless Scottish schiltrons rolled forward, spearing all those that they found. The Carse became a slaughter ground.

It was all over by noon. Not a living Englishman was left on the Carse, and the Scots got on with the time-honoured business of looting the enemy's camp and stripping the dead.

The number of casualties suffered by the two sides at Bannockburn have proved to be as controversial as the size of the armies that marched into battle. Among the nobles known to have been killed were Gloucester, Argentine, Clifford, Baron Lovel, John Comyn, William Marshal and Lord Litcham, while Bruce held as prisoners Baron Segrave, Baron Berkeley, Baron Montherme and Sir Ingelram Umfraville. Hereford was captured a few days later when he approached Bothwell Castle only to find it was in Scottish hands. Over 100 English knights are known to have been killed, plus perhaps as many as 600 esquires and mounted men at arms.

The death toll among the infantry must have been higher and figures of around 4,000 dead on the field seem reasonable, and more may have been killed in the days that followed. One modern analysis of the evidence suggests that as many as 11,000 English infantry were missing when the survivors mustered at Berwick some weeks later. However, some men are known to have gone home rather than head for Berwick. One unit of infantry from Gloucestershire is known to have crossed the border back into England at Carlisle. Their commander, Sir Maurice de Berkeley, boasted he had not lost a man on the long march south. Even so the English losses at Bannockburn were frightful.

King Edward himself got to Stirling Castle safely enough, along with Pembroke and other knightly fugitives. Castle governor Mowbray had been watching the disaster unfolding from the battlements of Stirling Castle with increasing dismay. He met Edward at the castle gates, but refused to let him enter. Mowbray knew that he would have to surrender the fortress to Bruce the next day. For Edward to enter the castle was merely to accept that he would soon be Bruce's prisoner.

Pembroke led Edward southwest, circling out west to avoid the Scottish army before heading southeast to Linlithgow and then on to Dunbar. There they found an English ship that carried the king and his exhausted bodyguard south to

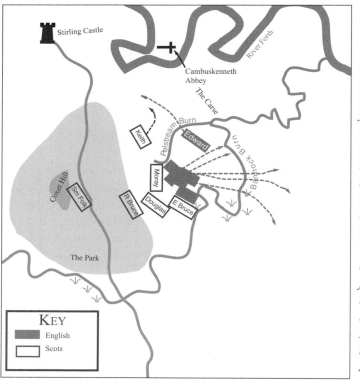

After several hours fighting King Edward II of England realised the battle could not be won and fled with his bodyguard toward Stirling Castle. His flight was the spark that led to the utter disintegration of the English army. The men turned and fled, only to find their escape route blocked by the Bannock Burn. Many never made it over the fatal stream.

Berwick and safety. He was humiliated, beaten and disgraced. For weeks Edward refused to appear in public, skulking in his private chambers with his favourites.

In contrast, Scottish losses were fairly light. Although it is difficult to be precise about losses among the infantry or light cavalry, only two knights are known to have been killed.

The route back across the Carse from the position of the most intense fighting must have looked invitingly open to the fleeing English, but just out of sight in the line of trees was the Bannock Burn, which would prove to be a difficult obstacle for armoured men to cross in a hurry. It trapped the English and allowed the pursuing Scots to turn the stream into a slaughter yard.

Chapter 6
Aftermath

The crushing victory of Robert Bruce at Bannockburn proved to be decisive. In time it delivered independence to Scotland and undisputed power to Robert Bruce.

The immediate effect of the Battle of Bannockburn was the surrender of Stirling Castle. Strictly speaking the castle had been relieved since some English fugitives did reach the castle after the battle, but in reality there was no hope of a genuine relief so Sir Philip Mowbray chose to stick to the original agreement. This was England's last stronghold in Scotland, other than Berwick which was captured soon after, so for the first time the northern kingdom was free of English garrisons.

The war, however, went on. Edward II had many problems in England, but he was not inclined to let Scotland slip from his grasp entirely. He seems to have been so overawed by the memory of his great father than he would not admit defeat in the north. Robert the Bruce led raids as far south as Lancashire and Yorkshire, even threatening York at one point, but Edward always managed to rally enough troops to drive him back without ever having enough to move into Scotland.

Finally in 1322 Edward led a new army into Scotland. This army was even larger than the one of 1314, but it achieved nothing. A new famine struck and the advancing army ran out of food. After the retreat to England Edward petulantly executed one of his commanders, the Earl of Carlisle, for having held talks with envoys from Robert Bruce. He then met those same envoys himself and agreed a truce to last 13 years.

England then collapsed into the civil war that had been threatening for so long. In January 1327 the Parliament and a gathering of nobles passed a motion calling on Edward to stand down so that his son, another Edward, could become king. Abandoned by his friends, surrounded by enemies and overwhelmed by emotion Edward agreed. Real power passed to his wife, Isabella, and her lover Roger

Mortimer. Edward died on 21 September 1327, murdered on the orders of Mortimer.

Isabella, acting in the name of Edward III, then agreed the Treaty of Northampton with Robert Bruce. The treaty stated that Scotland was a fully independent kingdom, that Robert Bruce was its king and that the border between England and Scotland would revert to that agreed between Alexander III of Scotland and Henry III of England. The Scots agreed to pay the English £100,000 in recompense. Peace came at last.

The other men who fought at Bannockburn enjoyed mixed fortunes.

Edward Bruce followed up the victory at Bannockburn with an invasion of Ireland. The situation in Ireland was complex with native kings and English nobles competing for lands, titles and powers. The ancient office of High King had fallen into abeyance, but Edward claimed it on the basis that several of his

The statue of Robert the Bruce that stands on the esplanade of Stirling Castle. The location was chosen so that the statue could look out over the site of King Robert's greatest military victory over the English. He is shown armed for battle while the Royal Arms of Scotland are carved on to the front of the plinth.

ancestors had held the title. The cause of the invasion was an appeal from Domhnall mac Briain Ó Néill, King of Tír Eóghain, who wanted help against English rivals and was willing to recognise Edward as High King in return.

Edward landed in Ireland with 6,000 men, announced that he was now High King of Ireland and summoned the subsidiary kings to do him homage. At first all went well as the Irish kings rallied to Edward as a means to get rid of the increasingly acquisitive English. But then famine struck and the Irish found that they had enough to do keeping their people alive without bothering with Edward's ambitions. In October 1318 Edward was defeated at Faughart by an army of English troops and allied Irish kings. He was killed in the fighting, his head was hacked off and sent to Edward II in England.

The Earl of Moray joined Edward Bruce on his ill fated expedition to Ireland, returning to Scotland in 1318. His later career was mostly taken up with diplomacy. He negotiated the Treaty of Corbeil with France, an important reaffirmation of the Auld Alliance. He then became Envoy to Rome. When Robert the Bruce died, Moray became Regent on behalf of Bruce's five year old son King David II. After three years of competent rule, Moray died of a sudden illness in July 1322. There were persistent rumours that he had been poisoned by an English agent, but no real proof.

The Black Douglas celebrated the victory at Bannockburn by leading a foray into northern England and for several years his life was devoted to border warfare. He captured Berwick in 1318, won the Battle of Myton in 1319 and played a key role in Bruce's victory at the Battle of Byland in 1322.

When Bruce died in 1329 he asked that Douglas carry his heart on crusade to Jerusalem. The heart was cut out and put into a silver casket which Douglas wore on a chain around his neck. Douglas and his band of Scottish knights got as far as Spain, where he found that King Alfonso XI of Castille was about to launch a war against the Moslems of Granada. Douglas joined the Christian army. In August 1330 Douglas won a large skirmish and was returning in triumph when he saw fellow Scot Sir William St Clair of Rosslyn surrounded by a force of Moslems. Douglas spurred to the rescue only to find his force trapped and outnumbered by over 20 to one. Realising he was doomed, Douglas tore the casket off his neck and threw it at the Moslems shouting "Now pass thou onward as thou wert wont, and Douglas will follow thee or die." He charged and was killed in the ensuing battle.

Walter the Steward married Robert Bruce's daughter Marjorie in 1315 and became Lord of Largs. After a relatively uneventful life he died in 1327. His son Robert later became King Robert II of Scotland, founding the Stewart (or Stuart) Dynasty.

On the English side, the Earl of Pembroke remained loyal to Edward II throughout the troubles that followed. He was instrumental in bringing the Earl of Lancaster to justice for the murder of Gaveston. Edward II was typically ungrateful, replacing Pembroke in several key positions with younger, more dashing men and doing nothing to help Pembroke when he fell into debt. On 24 June 1324 Pembroke had a seizure and died, being given a tomb in Westminster Abbey. Today he is probably best known as the founder of Pembroke College, Cambridge.

The Earl of Hereford led efforts to get Edward II to reform the government of England in the years that followed Bannockburn. The efforts came to nothing and in 1322 he joined the Earl of Lancaster in an open rebellion against Edward. The rebellion was crushed, and both earls killed, at the Battle of Boroughbridge. Hereford's body was treated like that of a traitor, but his son John was allowed to inherit his titles and estates.

Henry Beaumont went on to become one of the few men in the medieval period who could justifiably be called a military genius, though sadly he did not live long enough to enjoy the fruits of his work. After Bannockburn he was permanently deprived of his lands and titles in Scotland by Robert Bruce, and spent most of the rest of his life trying to get them back. After legal moves failed, he joined with other disinherited nobles in supporting the claims to the Scottish throne of Edward Balliol, son of the former king John Balliol. When Edward II refused to support "King Edward" of Scotland, Beaumont joined in the coup that saw Edward II overthrown and murdered. The new English government was no more inclined to help so Beaumont joined a new rebellion and when that failed fled into exile. In 1332 he persuaded Edward Balliol and some of his fellow dispossessed nobles to invade Scotland. It was largely through Beaumont's leadership that the invaders won the Battle of Dupplin Moor and put Balliol on the throne. Beaumont triumphantly took possession of his old lands and estates, but Balliol was ousted in 1336. Once again Beaumont lost his earldom and went into exile.

He went to England where news of his exploits had already made him famous. What Beaumont had done at Dupplin Moor was to develop entirely new tactical dispositions which saw knights dismount to fight on foot, men at arms draw up in dense phalanxes and archers put into dense formations of their own. By a skilful combination of different arms, each playing a different role and coming into play at different times, Beaumont revolutionized how warfare was conducted in western Europe. His new methods dominated warfare until firearms became both reliable and numerous in the early 16th century. After advising the new English king Edward III in the new style of warfare he moved to the Low Countries where he had relatives, and died in 1340. His daughter Isabel married Henry Duke of Lancaster in 1337 and through her was an ancestor of King Henry IV and so of the modern British Royal Family.

Sir Thomas Grey was released by the Scots after payment of ransom in 1316. Edward II then made him Constable of Norham Castle, a post he held for the next 20 years. During that time Grey withstood two prolonged Scottish sieges and retired with his honour and reputation intact. He died in 1344. Grey's son, another Sir Thomas, found fame in he 1350 when he wrote a history of England, which gave valuable detail on the Scottish wars drawn from first hand accounts of events by his father and his comrades as well as from his own experiences.

Philip Mowbray, the governor of Stirling Castle, was taken prisoner. He decided to join Edward Bruce's expedition to Ireland and was killed in battle at Faughart in 1318.

ALSO AVAILABLE IN THIS SERIES

The Battle of Wimbledon 568
The Battle of Crug Mawr 1136
The Battle of Lincoln 1141
The Battle of Lewes 1264
The Battle of Chesterfield 1266
The Battle of Bannockburn 1314
The Battle of Brighton 1377
The Battle of Northampton 1460
The Battle of Towton 1461
The Battle of Losecoat Field 1470
The Battle of Bosworth 1485
The Sieges of Newark 1643-46
The Siege of Leicester 1645